Sir Jeff's Birthday Treat

Written by
Jill Atkins

Illustrated by
Andy Hamilton

Sir Jeff was a knight. This was a happy day for him.

"It's my birthday!" he thought. "I hope I get a birthday treat."

At that moment, there was a knock on the window. Sir Jeff tried to picture who might be outside.

Then he opened the window.

He listened. There was a rustling that sounded like wrapping paper.

Sir Jeff called out. "Is that a birthday treat for me?"

"No," came the reply. "It's an order from the king."

Sir Jeff looked out. He could see his father, Sir Richard, with his long red hair and bristles.

Sir Richard held out a sheet of paper. Sir Jeff read what was written on it.

"His Majesty demands to see Sir Jeff at once."

"Did I do something wrong?" asked Sir Jeff. His knees began to knock.

"I don't know," said Sir Richard. "You must get ready."

Sir Jeff's fingers shook. His laces were in a knot and he could not fasten his helmet.

Then he began to bite his nails and gnaw his knuckles.

This was not the birthday treat he was expecting!

They galloped to the castle.

When they got there, Sir Jeff knelt at the king's feet.

"You sent for me, Sire," said Sir Jeff. "Did I do something wrong?"

The king frowned and folded his arms.

"Crumbs!" thought Sir Jeff. "The king is very cross with me."

"Sir Jeff," said the king. "The Blue Knight wants to fight with you in a contest."

Sir Jeff gulped. A contest! That meant a jousting match. It would be his first joust!

The king waved to his footman, who blew a whistle.

In rode a knight, dressed in blue from head to toe. Even his badge was blue.

Sir Jeff shook from head to toe. "I must be brave," he thought. "I'll do my best."

A crowd had gathered at the jousting field.

Everyone stamped and shouted as Sir Jeff and the Blue Knight approached.

Drums banged and whistles blew. Then the queen fluttered a flag.

That was the sign!

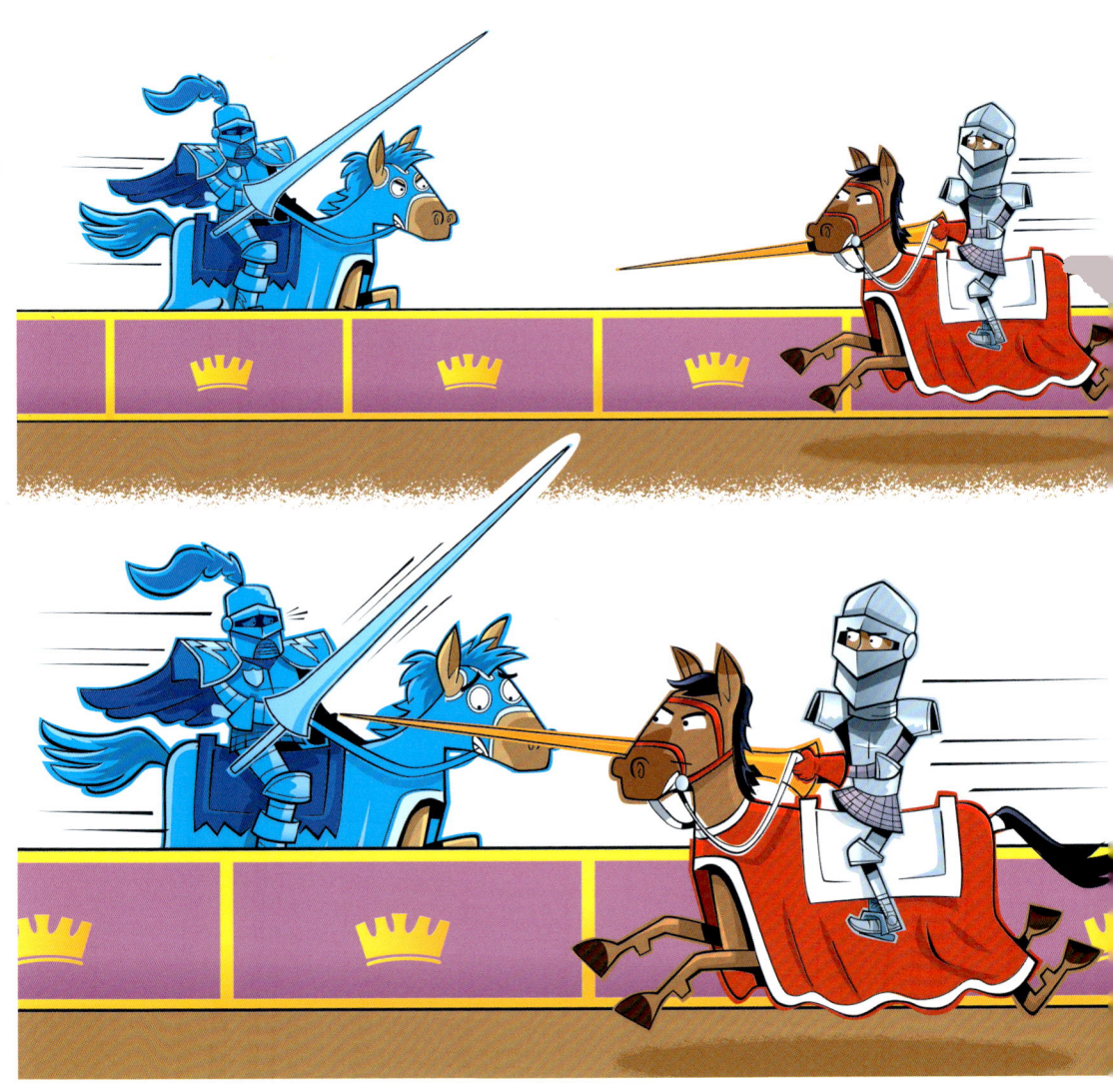

Sir Jeff galloped as fast as he could.

He lifted his weapon and pointed it at the Blue Knight.

Crash! Clatter! Clang!

The weapon struck the Blue Knight and he flew into the air. He landed in a heap. He was a wreck!

"You win!" he shouted, as Sir Jeff rode away.

"Wow!" said Sir Jeff. "I enjoyed that!"

"I'm glad," laughed the king. "I knew you would win. It was my birthday treat for you. Happy birthday, Sir Jeff!"

"Thank you, Sire!" laughed Sir Jeff, as he took a big bite of birthday cake.